W9-AVW-928

# Only At Night We See The Stars

CHIARA LUBICH

# ONLY AT NIGHT WE SEE THE STARS

## Finding Light in the Face of Darkness

New City Press

Published in the United States by New City Press
202 Cardinal Rd., Hyde Park, NY 12538
www.newcitypress.com
©2002 New City Press

Text selections are based on
*Erst in der Nacht sieht man die Sterne*
©1999 Neue Stadt, Munich, Germany
All texts have been newly translated from the original Italian
(see Sources, p. 87) by the NCP editorial staff

Cover design by Nick Cianfarani

   Library of Congress Cataloging-in-Publication Data:
Lubich, Chiara, 1920-
     [Selections. English. 2001]
     Only at night we see the stars : finding light in the face
of darkness / Chiara Lubich.
        p. cm.
     "Newly translated from the original Italian ... by the NCP
editorial staff"-- T.p. verso.
     ISBN 1-56548-158-5
     1. Suffering--Religious aspects--Catholic Church--
Meditations.   I. Title.

     BX2373.S5 L78 2001
     242--dc21                                    00-051105

Printed in Canada

# Contents

## Encounter

## Abandoned

## Maturing

# Foreword

To be given access to the interior thoughts, desires, and struggles of another human being is a privileged moment, one demanding reverence and utmost responsibility. Personal revelation is serious business, and when the issues involve such themes as suffering and joy, the mystery of grace and sin, the identity of God and the Lord Jesus, then we can be assured that the conversation will be challenging and revolutionary. If one is not up to conversion then it would be well to set this volume down now.

But for those who are yearning for spiritual growth and insight into God's word and the meaning of human existence, these prayer-filled reflections by Chiara Lubich will be most helpful. It is obvious that these meditations are based on two things: the word of God and the person of Jesus Christ. It is sacred scripture that records God's salvific activity throughout history and in our lives. It is the person of Jesus, crucified and abandoned, who reveals God's infinite love and mercy.

Chiara Lubich and the members of the Focolare Movement have given their lives over to living God's word in union with Jesus.

What makes this volume so necessary and essential in our times is its honest and courageous dealing with suffering and death. With deceptive simplicity and amazing boldness, *Only At Night We See the Stars* presents the gospel paradox of life coming through death. Because of Jesus, suffering plays a redemptive role on the path to Christian maturity, indeed, an essential function. And, as is so clearly stated, this is not a joyless suffering. Since we are united to Jesus in suffering and death, there is a deep joy that nothing can destroy.

This is not a book to be read. It is a spiritual manual to be prayed and pondered. Here is a wine which, if sipped slowly and lovingly, will lead to divine intoxication. It will also call us to the justice and peace that characterizes the followers of Jesus.

Robert F. Morneau
Auxiliary Bishop of Green Bay

# *Trust*

---

Scripture says,
"Cast all your cares on him"
(1 Pt 5:7)


All — even your own . . .

# In God's hand

Often we are tormented by thoughts
of what the future might hold.
But . . . "Each day has enough
trouble of its own" (Mt 6:34).

Tomorrow is another day,
and we shall then
face tomorrow's troubles.
We need not worry;
everything is in God's hands.
He will allow only his will
to be accomplished,
and this is always for our good.

# Life's golden thread interrupted

A sudden misfortune
reminds us of the words of scripture,
"Everything is vanity of vanities"
(Eccl 1:2).
Yes, everything passes:
people, health, beauty, possessions.
God alone remains.

Misfortunes
*can* mark the time for us
to choose God anew
as the one and all of our life,
and thus live the way he commands:
to love.

When you love,
you understand many things,
and you will see

how the golden thread of your life,
at first apparently interrupted,
continues to shine as brightly
and even more so than before.

In our lives
we might experience
all kinds of disruptions,
but the life of God
is always alive,
and so it is in those
who have grafted themselves
over and over onto him.

# Life is hard

Jesus invites us:
"Come to me, all you
who are weary and oppressed,
and I will restore you" (Mt 11:28).

How comforting these words are!
The gospels,
the books of scripture,
are also books of consolation,
and it would be false pride,
even inhuman, to deny it.

Let us openly admit
that we suffer here on earth
and that life is hard!
Does this suffering not call
for a consoler?

Yes, life is hard.
But God who is love knows it.

He has always thought of us:
First by promising the Messiah
from the world's beginning,
and then by giving us the Messiah.
For one who believes,
this answers everything.
And balance is restored.

## Only today's troubles

God is generous in everything.
But when it comes to suffering,
the Lord says,
"Each day has enough trouble
of its own" (Mt 6:34).

We know that he does not deceive us.
So if we follow his will
and concern ourselves
only with today's troubles,
the worries we were expecting tomorrow
may never actually happen.

## Yes to his will

God knows the road we should take at every point of our lives. For each of us he has fixed a celestial orbit for the star of our freedom to travel. But we must abandon ourselves to him, our creator. We each have our own orbit, our own life that does not conflict with the orbits plotted for billions of others, offspring of the same Father as we. Ours harmonizes with theirs in a firmament more splendid than that of the stars, because it is spiritual.

God must manage our life and guide it into the divine adventure we cannot foresee, but where moment to moment we offer the contribution of our free will, at once spectators and protagonists, in wonderful scenarios of love.

We *can* offer our will, freely and lovingly; not, we *ought to* offer it or, what is worse, resign ourselves to offering it.

God is a Father,
and therefore he is love.
He is the creator,
our redeemer,
and our sanctifier.
Who better than he
knows what is good for us?

# Realistic and hopeful

"Affliction makes for endurance,
and endurance for tested virtue,
and tested virtue for hope.
And this hope will not
leave us disappointed."
                    (Rom 5:3-5)

I find this sentence of scripture enchanting. Paul takes us from tribulation to patience, from patience to experience, from experience to hope, all for things above . . . but also for here below.

And this does have its logic. It is the logic of the supernatural life. If in the challenges of daily life we continue to love, things become clear within and wc receive the light to understand.

Experiencing this helps us not to lose heart or to fool ourselves, not to fall into depression or to be overly elated. And from this in turn comes the hope that we will receive what has been promised in the next life, and on this earth the hundredfold.

What we thus learn from experience gives us hope. It is a light that shines as though through the knots sewn on one side of a tapestry by the tribulations of each day, revealing its design on the other.

And so, hope that springs forth from the supernatural life in us is a sublime virtue, so close to charity itself.

Not by chance, Paul continues and says, ". . . hope will not leave us disappointed, because the love of God has been poured out in our hearts through the Holy Spirit who has been given to us" (Rom 5:5).

## Someone listens to us

Jesus knows everything.
He reads our hearts,
knows our thoughts.
How consoling to be sure of this,
when for example
from the bottom of our hearts
we ask him for favors or praise him
or want to express our love for him.
He knows it; he perceives it all.

Think of the encounter of Thomas
and the risen Christ:
Jesus knew everything about Thomas.
He knew that Thomas
wanted to put his finger
into the nail marks
and his hand into Jesus' side.
Jesus, who is God,
knows everything.

What a comfort for those who pray.
God does listen to us,
and this is enough for us.
Whether or not
he then grants our request
is not the point;
after all, he knows
what is good for us.
Thomas replies
with the wonderful words,
"My Lord and my God!" (Jn 20:28),
and these same words
also spring from our hearts
as we read this gospel passage.

# Carried

---

We don't have to carry
our cross alone;
God carries it with us.

## When the shadow of suffering arrives . . .

When suffering overshadows our life, we are brought back to reality, that is, natural and supernatural life. In such moments we return more easily to God, should we have wandered away a little. When suffering is lacking, instead, we often delude ourselves with what is transitory.

However, suffering should not fill our soul with bitterness, preventing us from seeing the gifts God bestows on us day by day. For it is characteristic of the Christian to have the hundredfold in this life, even in the midst of persecutions (cf. Mk 10:30).

God wants us to thank him for both the hundredfold and for the suffering, and so our heart should be open to both.

We need to understand that the cross is essential to our Christian life. If we accept it, suffering loses its heaviness, it becomes light and easy, and takes its rightful place. We don't have to carry it alone. In fact, God carries it with us.

Thus we will be able to recognize the beauty and the consolation that accompanies our daily pain. Suffering, then, has a very important function; it helps us stay in a supernatural attitude.

## In need of our neighbor

When we need our neighbor's care,
let us not feel humiliated.
Let us even then be aware
of our own dignity,
and with all our heart
thank whoever is helping us.
But the greatest thanks
we reserve for God,
who has made
the human heart charitable;
and for Christ,
who by announcing the Good News
with his own blood,
especially his new commandment,
has stimulated countless souls
to help one another.

# Reverence for those who suffer

Whoever suffers and is in darkness
sees further than one
who is not suffering.
The sun has to set
before we see the stars.

Suffering teaches
what cannot be learned
in any other way.
It holds the highest rank,
the teacher of wisdom.
And whoever has wisdom is blessed
(cf. Prv 3:13).

"Blessed are those who suffer,
for they shall be comforted" (Mt 5:4)
— not only with their reward
in the next life
but also with the contemplation
of heavenly things here on earth.

We should approach
those who suffer
with the same
and even more reverence
than we used
to approach our elders,
sure that from them
we would receive great wisdom.

## Who shows compassion?

Lord, give me
all those who are lonely. . . .
My heart has felt
the passionate desire
which invades yours
over the abandoned state
in which the whole world
is immersed.

I feel love for everyone
who is sick and alone.
Whom do they have
to comfort their tears?
Who shows compassion
for them in their slow death?
Who hugs to their own heart
the heart in despair?

O my God,
grant that I may be in the world
a tangible sacrament of your love;
let me be your arms,
hugging to myself
all the loneliness in the world
and consuming it with love.

## Precious pearl

The "precious pearl" (cf. Mt 13:45f) —
is it not Jesus himself,
who gave himself up
on the cross (cf. Phil 2:7f),
in highest poverty
and absolute emptiness?

If we let him live in us,
we are nothing but love.
No longer do we live,
but he lives in us (cf. Gal 2:20),
and thus God's will for us
comes to fulfillment.

Then we do not live for ourselves,
and we can be love for others.
We are empty,
and others can pour out
whatever they may have
in their hearts.

The one who is thus freed
from distress and pressing worries,
is open to God's love.
Seed placed in such a heart,
falls on good ground.
In this way
the kingdom spreads,
the only one worth building up:
God's kingdom.
For this we pray each day.

## The power of love

Have you ever noticed
a little blade of grass,
caressed by the winds of spring,
that has broken through the surface
of an abandoned road?
Life, insuppressible,
is reborn.

And it is the same
in the humanity surrounding you,
if you're careful not to look at it
through worldly eyes,
but restore it with love's divine rays.

The supernatural love
from your heart
is like sunshine,
which permits no postponement
to life's return.

It is a life that forms the cornerstone
for your own corner in life.
Nothing more is needed
to pick the world up
and restore it to God.

# Letting go

If one day
our sufferings
should reach such intensity
that everything in us
rebels against our pain
because the very fruit
of our "passion"
seems to be withdrawn
from our hands
and even from our hearts,
then let us remember
Mary Desolate.

It is this anguish
which will make us
resemble her more closely;
it is through this anguish
that the figure of Mary
will emerge more clearly
in our lives:

Mary,
all-beautiful,
mother of everyone
because she is detached
from everyone,
most of all
from her divine Son
because of God's divine will.

## You on the cross

We would simply die
if we did not fix our gaze on you.
As if magically,
you transform every bitterness
into sweetness:
We see you brought
to a complete standstill
as you cry out from the cross
in absolute inactivity,
in a living death.

You hurled all your fire
upon the earth
as you yourself turned cold
and, finishing your life there,
you flung infinite,
endless life into us,
who live it now with elation.

We want nothing more
than to see ourselves like you,
at least a little,
joining our pain to yours
and offering it to the Father.

## Your tears

Jesus was "troubled in spirit"
and "began to weep."
The gospel says it (Jn 11:35.33).

Jesus!
Your weeping consoles us.
In your tears
we find our own.
You will be patient with us
and with our tears,
because you yourself have wept.
Wherever you see tears,
you recognize yourself.

## Silent pain

If one day we feel useless,
with nowhere to go
and written off by others,
and this seems absurd to our soul
and even more so to our heart,
which protests, and rightly so,
then let us remember Jesus forsaken.

Also this, our silent and nameless pain,
is contained in the many facets
of his suffering.

## Condemned to inactivity?

If you are suffering,
and your kind of suffering
puts a halt to everything
you would be doing,
think of the Mass.
In the Mass,
today just like then,
Jesus is neither working
nor preaching:
He is sacrificing himself
out of love.

There are so many things
that could be done in a lifetime,
so many things to say;
but however silent
and inaudible to others,
the voice of pain,
offered for love,
speaks the loudest.

It pierces heaven.
If you are suffering,
plunge your pain into his:
Offer your own Mass,
and don't let it trouble you
if the world does not understand.
It is enough that Jesus, Mary,
and the saints understand you.
Live with them,
and shed your blood
for the good of humanity,
as he did.

The Mass!
It is beyond our understanding!
His Mass, and ours.

# *E*ncounter

What a desert
surrounds us at times.
But when you are present,
we find ourselves in a sea of peace.

# You are there!

I have met you
in such a variety of places, Lord.

I've heard your heartbeat
in the deep stillness
of a mountain chapel,
in the dim light
of an empty cathedral's
sanctuary lamp,
and in the chorus
of a crowd that loves you,
and fills the arches of your church
with love and song.
I have met you in joy.
I have spoken with you
beyond the starry firmament,
while I came home from work
in the evening, in silence.

I seek you, and find you often.
But where I always find you
is in pain.
Any pain whatsoever
is like the sound of a bell
summoning God's spouse to prayer.

When the shadow
of the cross approaches,
the soul recollects herself
in her secret tabernacle,
oblivious of the ringing of the bell
she "sees" you and talks to you.
You have come to my door,
I have come to answer:
"I'm here, Lord,
it's you who I want,
it's you I long for."

At this encounter
my soul, all but inebriated
with your love,
does not feel its pain,
I, suffused with you,
carrying you within me:
I in you, you in me,
that we may be one.
Then I reopen
my eyes to life,
to the less true life,
using all you have taught me
for the battle to be waged
in your name.

## Like the ringing of a bell

Lord,
I thank you
for your visiting us in suffering.
Because when we suffer
we meet you face to face.

When the pain is strong
our soul is attracted to God
and longs for union with him.

A bare cross,
chasms and storms . . .
If we love all this as our one and all
in it we will find a sun
that does not set:
God who is love,
who has called us,
and who loved us so much.

## Not suffering but love

It is not true
that one who loves the cross,
as Christ has commanded us to do,
finds suffering.

One who carries it willingly
even when it is hard
finds love instead,
finds God.

## A unique strategy

I've noticed
your strategy is consistent
but never monotonous.
Maybe it is because
you *are* your own action.
You are love that is always new.

This is your strategy:
When souls are satisfied with shadows
(and I'm not speaking of mortal
shadows, but when their life
is lived for you but is not you),
often you send pain.

The soul then comes back
and says its yes to you.
There are times
when that yes is fragranced
with a feeling of profound gratitude
and plunges into a singular prayer:

"Yes Lord,
when I meet your cross
I find you there.
Thank you
for calling me back to yourself
and not only
to what are your concerns,
because I am drawn
to solitude with you
more than to anything else,
to the same solitude
I shall be obliged to face anyway
on the day when we meet
if I do not choose it now with love.

"May you,
who can do all things,
procure for me in your name
the grace to arrive
at that continual conversation

between you-in-me and you,
where events, people, and things
are nothing but fuel for our pure love."

This alone is true life,
because it is a spark of yours,
of you yourself:
a life without deception
or disappointments,
with no interruptions and no sunset.

## A pathway through the desert

Lord,
what a desert surrounds us at times.
But we will get there; we're on the way.
We do not know
how long our journey will be.
But we do not want to live
as if we will remain here forever.
Each day we travel a little further;
we rest and resume the journey
the following day,
drawing ever closer to you,
though we know not our final hour.

Lord,
you promise all things
to those who ask with faith.
Grant that we may arrive
only on the day
in which your plan for us is fulfilled.

Grant this to everyone we love,
and to all people,
so that soon we will all meet again,
united with you
and with your mother and ours
when the evening of this precious day,
life itself, has set.

# All and nothing

The smallest thing
that goes wrong in our bodies
places us in front of consequences
ranging from almost nothing
to something serious,
even life-threatening.

In moments like these
our world once again
crumbles before us.
We find ourselves
before the One
who is Everything: God.

And in him we find
what the ideal of our Christian life
has formed in us day to day,
that splendor of light

which in every life situation
calls for love and fullness of life,
even in moments
of painful illness or surgery
or, for that matter,
in the face of death.

As strange as it might sound,
I have experienced it,
and only then I understood:
*Nothingness* coincides with the *All*.
I lack *nothing* because I have
the *all* I want.

# *A*bandoned

Jesus cried with a loud voice,
"My God, my God,
why have you forsaken me?"

# For me

Speaking of Jesus, Paul writes, ". . . and he gave his life for me" (Rom 5:8). Each of us can repeat those words of the apostle: *for me*.

My Jesus,
you have died for me,
how can I doubt your mercy?
And if I can believe in that mercy
with a faith that teaches me
that God has died for me,
how can I not risk everything
to return such love?

*For me* . . .
Words that wipe away
the solitude of the most lonely
and give divine value
to every person despised by the world.
Words that fill every heart

and make it overflow upon those
who either do not know
or do not remember the Good News.

*For me.*
For me, Jesus, all those sufferings?
For me that cry on the cross?
Surely, you will never give up on us.
You will do everything imaginable
to save us if only
because we have cost you so much.

You gave me divine life
just as my mother gave me human life.
In every moment
you think of me alone,
as you do of each and every person.
This — more than anything
in the world — gives us the courage
to live as Christians.

*For me.* Yes, for me.
And so, Lord,
for the years that remain,
allow me also to say:
*for you.*

## For us

So that we might have the light,
you made yourself darkness.

To acquire union for us,
you experienced separation
from the Father.

So that we might have wisdom,
you made yourself ignorance.

To clothe us in innocence,
you became sin.

So that God might be present in us,
you felt him far away from you.

# Transformation

I would like to bear witness
to the whole world
that Jesus forsaken
has filled every void,
illumined all darkness,
accompanied all loneliness,
annulled every pain,
wiped out every sin.

## My one and all

"I determined that while I was with you I would speak of nothing but Jesus Christ and him crucified" (1 Cor 2:2).

I have only one Spouse on earth:
Jesus forsaken.
I have no God but him.
In him is the whole of paradise
with the Trinity
and the whole of the earth
with humanity.
Therefore what is *his* is mine,
and nothing else.
And *his* is universal suffering,
and therefore mine.
I will go through the world
seeking it in every instant of my life.
What hurts me is *mine*.
Mine the suffering that grazes me
in the present.

Mine the suffering of the souls beside
me (that is my Jesus).
*Mine* all that is not peace,
not joy, not beautiful,
not loveable, not serene,
in a word, what is not paradise.
Because I too have *my* paradise,
but it is that in my Spouse's heart.
I know no other.
So it will be for the years I have left:
athirst for suffering, anguish, despair,
sorrow, exile, forsakenness, torment—
for all that is him,
and he is sin, hell.

In this way
I will dry up the waters of tribulation
in many hearts nearby
and, through communion

with my almighty Spouse,
in many faraway.
I shall pass as a fire
that consumes all that must fall
and leaves standing only the truth.
But it is necessary to be like him:
to be him in the present moment of life.

# *Maturing*

The fire of love
we reach only
by passing through
the ice of suffering.

## Passage

Covered by a mantle of snow
the grain of wheat
develops underground.

Isolated by a layer of abandonment
we grow
in union with God.

# Even amidst tears

The cross, especially one of prolonged suffering, is one of the greatest gifts that God can send us. Immersed in that suffering, as though transported into the darkness above the atmosphere, our vision of the vast universe is made clearer.

When the cross is lacking instead, we may easily mistake fireflies for stars. We might think that all we do is in God's service, compatible with and even useful for his glory, but all the while we cater to our own ego and vanity. As a result, we offer God a life that mixes smoke with incense.

When, on the other hand, suffering comes to visit us and stays for a long time, we might understand the saints' words that speak of a life away from the limelight, of self-denial and of authenticity before God and our fellow human beings.

Such a realization can be so strong as to cause one even to offer acts of gratitude to the One who permits suffering.

The cross certainly brings us to the right path and is the guarantee that the roots of our life are expanding: the sign of new beauty about to blossom.

And we start to realize that the beatitudes are not merely promises or encouragements but a reality. One who weeps can really find blessings in this very weeping. It is a true beatitude, though not yet the one to come in eternity.

# The roots

The width
of a tree's foliage
often corresponds
to that of its roots.

Similarly,
Christ's love
expands our hearts
through the measure
of the pain
we have suffered for
and offered to him.

## Unexpected hope

At times,
we feel plunged
into such spiritual anguish
that darkness is all around us,
everything is a torment,
and not a single ray of light
penetrates our life
to lift us up. . . .

But then,
when we least expect it,
God reveals himself. . . .
We gain new hope. . . .
God speaks to us
of something long forgotten:
mercy, peace.

## Mercy over sacrifice

When one has known pain in all its cruel nuances, in its various forms of anguish, and has reached out to God in agonized, speechless supplication, in meek cries for help; when one has drained the chalice to its dregs, for days or years offering one's own cross to God, fused with his (which gives ours divine value), then comes the time when God takes pity on us and takes us into union with him.

At this moment, when the unique value of pain has been learned by experience, and one has come to believe in the economy of the cross, having seen its beneficent effects, the Lord reveals in a new and higher form something worth even more than pain.

This is love of our neighbor in the form of mercy, the kind of love which opens our heart and arms to the wretched, the needy, to those who have been broken by life, to the repentant sinners.

The sort of love that can take in all who have lost their way, be they friend, brother or sister, or stranger, and never stops forgiving. Love which celebrates the return of a sinner more than it does a thousand righteous, lending to God our intelligence and the goods necessary to be able to show joy to the prodigal son at his return.

A love that doesn't measure and will not be measured.

This is love grown more abundant, more universal, and more concrete than what the soul had before. It even feels the rise of sentiments resembling those of Jesus; it notices divine words surfacing on its own lips for whomever it meets: "My heart is moved with pity for the crowd" (Mt 15:32). Mercy is the ultimate expression of love, what caps it off. Love surpasses pain, which belongs only to this life; love carries on into the next. The Lord prefers mercy to sacrifice (cf. Mt 9:32).

# The paradox of suffering

In our daily duties there are always burdensome  elements which entail some measure of fatigue and discomfort. But these are the very things that we should appreciate as precious gifts that we can offer to God.

Everything that tastes of suffering is, in fact, of utmost importance. The world does not accept suffering, because it is no longer familiar with the value Christian life gives it, and because suffering goes against our human nature. Thus, the world tries to avoid and to ignore it.

Yet, suffering has a mysterious task: It can become a way to happiness, to that true and enduring happiness which alone can fill our hearts. It is the same happiness that God enjoys and that we humans, destined to what is absolute, can share already in this life.

Precisely through his suffering, Jesus has given joy to every person: joy here on earth and unending joy in the next life. In the same way, by accepting and offering to him our daily worries and concerns, we obtain happiness for ourselves and for others.

# Joy

Christian joy
is like a ray of light
shining through a tear drop;
it is like a flower
that blossoms from a pool of blood;
it is the essence of love
distilled from suffering.

This is why Christian joy is unique,
with a totally new dimension
and an apostolic force
which reveals a glimpse of paradise.

## Peace

Peace, Lord.
What a great conquest peace is!
For your gift of peace,
a person would rather endure
many physical sufferings
than lose peace again.
Because all suffering combined
does not measure up
to a life without peace.

Peace is a fruit of the spirit.
But to acquire it
we have to do our part.
We need to transform
torment, anguish,
inner struggles,
moments of aridity,
turmoil and temptation,
into occasions to love God.

## Not only pain

It is not true, Lord,
that all of our life is suffering.
It is not true, Lord,
that the cross embitters
and overshadows
all the days of our existence.

Certainly,
for those who love you, Lord,
suffering plays a great
and irreplaceable role.
But it is not the only thing
we encounter in following you.
As we follow you,
above all we see you.
You are love,
and you change
every suffering into joy,
a joy that makes us proceed
with a hundredfold of ardor.

## Toward the goal

Joy and suffering,
consolation and affliction,
repentance and resurrection;
some things simply permitted by God
and others clearly willed by him;
conquests and painful losses;
acclaim and criticism;
slow furthering of works
for God's glory,
and the blossoming of new life
in the midst of weeds. . . .

If we love the Lord,
everything has only one destiny,
one single purpose:
to lead us to union with God.

# Sources

The selected texts in this book have been taken and newly translated from the following works by Chiara Lubich, all published by Città Nuova, Rome (numbers refer to page numbers in this book, followed by the page number in the Italian original):

*Scritti spirituali/1 (L'attrattiva del tempo moderno)*, 1991:
11:261; 16:234; 17:101; 29:59; 32:35; 36:74; 40:41; 43:142; 44:47; 49:78/79; 52:139/141; 53:132; 54:96; 57:246-247; 66:41; 67:44; 68:45; 73:228; 76:232; 77:260; 78:66/67; 84:285; 85:224; 86:225

*Scritti spirituali/2 (L'essenziale di oggi)*, 1984:
12:186; 14:60; 19:38; 22:209; 27:181; 30:78; 34:166; 38:242; 42:47; 59:22; 63:11; 74:193; 81:167; 83:181